APERTURE

WITH PHOTOGRAPHS BY:

Maarten Vanden Abeele, Juan Carlos Alom, Alexander Apóstol, David Armstrong, Eve Arnold, Richard Avedon, Tina Barney, Letizia Battaglia, Cecil Beaton, Claude Cahun, Elinor Carucci, Helen Chadwick, Marianne Courville, Gregory Crewdson, Imogen Cunningham, Bruce Davidson, Jesse DeMartino, Baron Adolf de Meyer, Philip-Lorca diCorcia, Elliot Erwitt, Paul Fusco, Anna Gaskell, Robert Gligorov, Burt Glinn, Nan Goldin, Janine Gordon, Peter Hujar, Mimmo Jodice, Seydou Keïta, Gyorgy Kepes, Barbara Kruger, Jacques-Henri Lartigue, Clarence John Laughlin, Annie Leibovitz, Man Ray, Robert Mapplethorpe, Mary Ellen Mark, Will McBride, Ana Mendieta, Tracey Moffatt, Mariko Mori, Yasumasa Morimura, Shirin Neshat, Nic Nicosia, Nicholas Nixon, John O'Reilly, Luigi Ontani, Jaime Palacios, Adrian Piper, Sylvia Plachy, Richard Prince, Miguel Rio Branco, Herb Ritts, Walter Rosenblum, Paolo Roversi, David Salle, Lucas Samaras, Gary Schneider, David Seymour, Cindy Sherman, Laurie Simmons, Lorna Simpson, Sandy Skoglund, Paul Strand, Dennis Stock, Laureana Toledo, Ronald Treager, David Wanderman, Andy Warhol, Carrie Mae Weems, Garry Winogrand

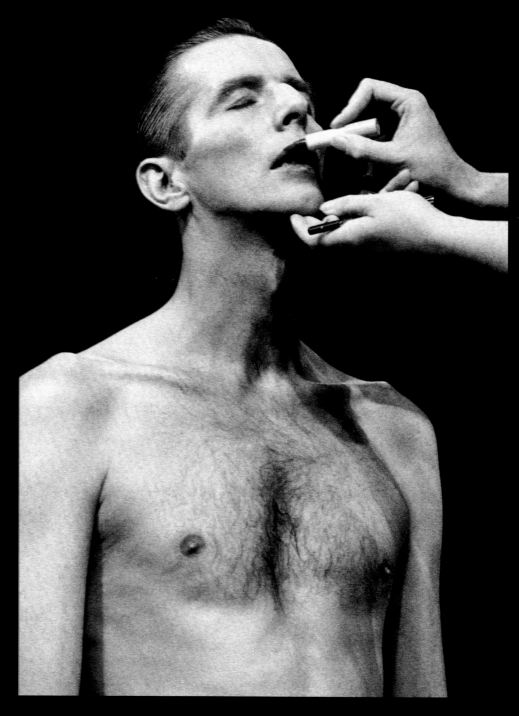

Perhaps a mind that is purely masculine cannot create,
any more than a mind that is purely feminine. . . .
It is fatal to be a man or woman pure and simple;
one must be woman-manly or man-womanly.

—VIRGINIA WOOLF, 1929

MALE ♂♀ FEMALE

Humankind's first and most essential dichotomy—that we are created in two natures, male and female—has fascinated artists for millenia. Each sex has suggested different powers and lures over the ages, but perhaps no era has explored the spectrum of gender with its nuances and variety as ours has. Inspired by the exhibition "Male," curated by Vince Aletti, and co-edited with Aletti, this issue of Aperture *combines more than one hundred images that utilize humor, intensive self-reflection, and iconic forms in their exploration of male/female. This visual dialog, along with a very personal introduction by Aletti, an intelligent and revealing interview with Madonna, and a wildly clever text by Wayne Koestenbaum articulates countless expressions of gender. We are grateful to Aletti for his creativity and generous collaboration.* —THE EDITORS

For as long as I can remember I have collected pictures: snapshots, film stills, pages torn from magazines, postcards, cartes de visite, studio portraits, stereo views, gallery announcements, club flyers, discarded Polaroids, tintypes, newspaper clippings, photobooth strips. This personal image bank, whether pushpinned to the wall or filed away in drawers and boxes, has become an ever-expanding frame of reference. At once a history and a time bomb rigged to go off with dependable regularity, this cache of idols and icons has the weight of memory, the volatility of desire. Images can be a consolation or a disturbance, an inspiration or a burden. We live through them; they live through us. Like the famously crowded, casually revealing bulletin boards of artists and designers—looking at Picasso's or Avedon's or Lagerfeld's is like discovering an open diary—my pictures tell a story I can't put into words, a story I don't entirely understand.

Mostly, it's a story about men and women, masculinity and femininity. Looking at pictures of men—of cowboys, sailors, boxers, models, musclebuilders, actors, painters; of Genet, Belmondo, de Kooning, Godard, Lew Alcindor, and Liam Gallagher—I wonder, Who do they think they are? And, inevitably, who do I think I am? Only the luckiest among us know immediately, instinctively where we fit in the world. Most of us grow up as wary observers, alert to the slightest movement in the social order, wondering where we belong, if we belong. In adolescence, a fluid identity is rarely an option, and eventually all but the most alienated find a place, and then another place; for better or worse, a lifetime of places.

But many of us remain perpetual outsiders when it comes to masculinity and feminin-ity. Gender, in most cases, is not an option; we are male or female: a given. But are we masculine or feminine? Even if we accept the notion that, ideally, we share both mas-

(continued on page 6)

Opposite: Maartin Vanden Abeele, *Lutz Förster in* 1980, choreography by Pina Bausch, Wuppertal, Germany, 1995

*To me gender
is not physical at all,
but is altogether
insubstantial. It is
soul, perhaps,
it is talent, it is taste,
it is environment,
it is how one feels,
it is light and shade,
it is inner music....
It is the essentialness
of oneself.*

—JAN MORRIS,
Conundrum, 1974

Jesse DeMartino, *Jason and Mike at
the Cabin Near Huntsville,* Texas, 1996

culine and feminine traits, what exactly are they? Who decides? Ultimately, of course, each of us does, but only after struggling with all the narrow, contradictory definitions we've absorbed over the years. Most of those definitions come to us not in words but in pictures, which are so much more persuasive and insidious. Even the most skeptical of viewers can't help but register the prevailing mode of masculinity or femininity and measuring themselves against it. But skepticism is rarely part of our intellectual repertoire when we begin forming our ideas about how men and women should act. No wonder, then, that masculinity/femininity can seem to be a straitjacket, a sham, a trap, a bad joke, a dead end.

None of this is new. We've been hasseling over these issues for decades now and redefining ourselves—sexually, socially, psychologically—in the process. The images that we test ourselves against have changed, becoming at once subtler and more blatant, but they're no less difficult to resist. Besides, the old images are still around, some more potent than ever. Brando in a white T-shirt, Marky Mark in white briefs, Marilyn Monroe with her skirt billowing up, Kate Moss lying nude on a velvet couch: icons-R-us. We love them; we hate them; we pretend not to care. Making things more complicated, advertising, like art, has incorporated gender critique, then palmed it back on us as parody, irony, and prepackaged outrage—shall I supersize it for you, sir?

Since most advertising can be more interesting—certainly more engaging—than some art, there's no point in resisting it. But giving in doesn't mean giving up. In fact, the more the better. While total immersion in the image world might be dangerously overstimulating, the accumulation of messages tends to both level out their individual power and play up their contradictions. So that Calvin Klein underwear model has to share psychic space with Boy George and Maxwell, Oscar de la Hoya and Malcolm X, the Marlboro Man and Rudolph Nureyev, Bill Clinton and Dennis Rodman. And the *Playboy* centerfold curls up alongside Aretha Franklin, Cindy Sherman, Edith Sitwell, Frida Kahlo, Jeanne Moreau, k.d. lang, Iman, your mama, and the girl next door. Every picture tells a different story; together, they begin to add up to a definition of masculinity or femininity, but only if they're understood in the plural: many masculinities, multiple femininities. More, more, more.

We can only begin to suggest that multiplicity in these pages. Think of this as a starting point, a map for further exploration. In the end, every definition of male and female is personal, and it's that idiosyncracy we value, need, and hope to encourage. Who do we think we are? A work in progress. ♂♀

—VINCE ALETTI

RA63095 P23-9

Richard Avedon, *Lew Alcindor, Basketball Player*, New York, May 2, 1963

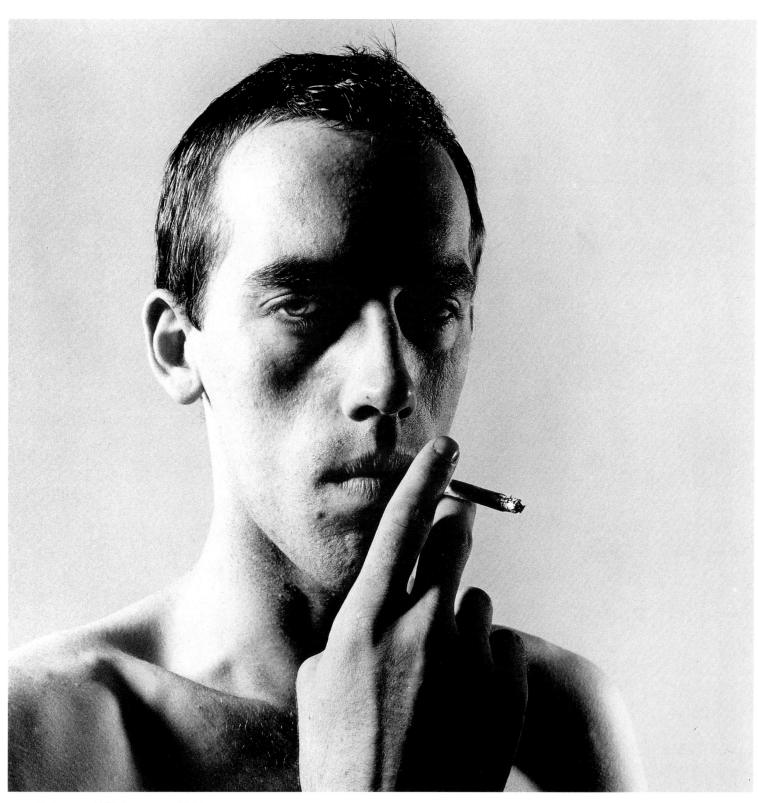

Peter Hujar, *David Wojnarowicz*, 1981

Janine Gordon, *Stripping on Clinton Street*, 1995

John O'Reilly, *Studio Portrait*, 1997

Walter Rosenblum, *Three Men, 105th Street*, New York, 1952

Seydou Keïta, *Untitled*, 1950

Lucas Samaras, untitled, 1996

Lucas Samaras, untitled, 1995

Gary Schneider, *Ueli*, 1995

Cecil Beaton,
Mick Jagger on the set
of *Performance*, 1968

Will McBride, *Washroom at the Salem School*, Lake Constance, Germany, 1968

Nan Goldin, *Honda Brothers in Cherry Blossom Storm*, Tokyo, 1994

Above: Tina Barney, *The Boys*, 1990. *Below*: Sylvia Plachy, *Alex's Bar Mitzvah*, 1982

Bruce Davidson, Newt Gingrich interviewed by John Barry Barlow in the Capitol, 1995

Sylvia Plachy, *Mikes*, 1981

Above: Nic Nicosia, #7, from the series "Real Pictures," 1987. *Opposite*: Marianne Courville, *Harry the Hunter*, 1968/1995

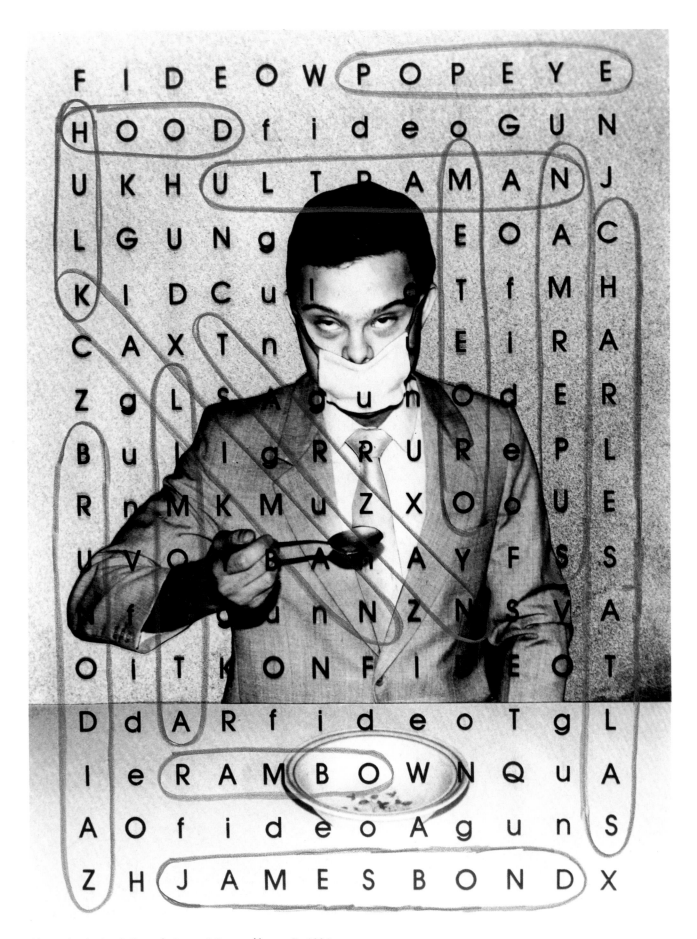

Alexander Apóstol, *Sopa de Letres I* (Soup of letters I), 1995

Tracey Moffatt

Charm Alone, 1965

His brother said, '*crooked nose and no chin –
you'll have to survive on charm alone*'.

Tracey Moffatt, *Charm Alone*, 1965, from the series "Scarred for Life," 1994

Juan Carlos Alom, *Untitled*, from the series "El Libro Oscuro" (The dark book), 1995

Cecil Beaton, *Portrait of Stephen Tennant*, 1930

Cecil Beaton, *The Hon. Stephen Tennant*, 1927–28

Baron Adolf de Meyer, *Portrait of Ernest*, 1938

David Armstrong, *Andrew as a Sailor*, New Haven, 1996

Richard Prince,
Untitled, 1980–86

30

Luigi Ontani, *Davide e Golia* (David and Goliath), Madras, 1977

Luigi Ontani, *Bacchino* (Bacchus), Bologna, 1972

Above: Luigi Ontani, *Leda e il cigno* (Leda and the swan), Mediterranean Sea, 1975
Below: Luigi Ontani, *Mille arti sulle spine* (A thousand limbs on thorns), 1975

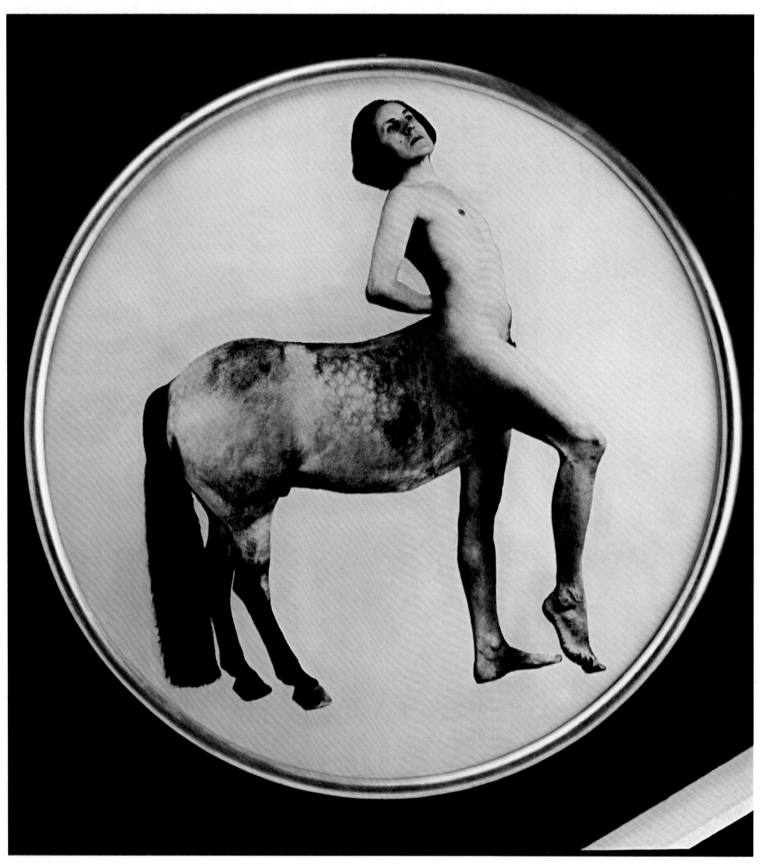

Luigi Ontani, *Centaur*, Rome, 1995

Above: Juan Carlos Alom, *Mitad del Mundo* (Half of the world), 1996. *Opposite*: Eve Arnold, Mikhail Baryshnikov at his daily class at the American Ballet Theatre, 1987

From top left, clockwise: Robert Mapplethorpe, *Ken Moody*, 1983. Robert Mapplethorpe, *Arnold Schwartzenegger*, 1976. Robert Mapplethorpe, *Torso*, 1987. Robert Mapplethorpe, *Untitled*, 1980. *Opposite*: Herb Ritts, *Fred with Tires*, from the series "Bodyshop," 1984

Michael Jordan in his trademark "Air Jordan" pose for a Nike advertisement, 1987

Miguel Rio Branco, *Sem* (Without), Santa Rosa, Rio de Janiero, 1992

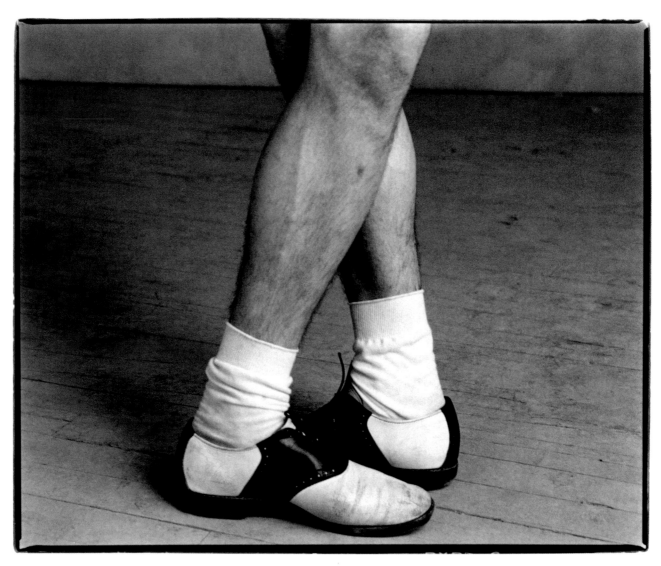

Annie Leibovitz, *Mark Morris*, 1990

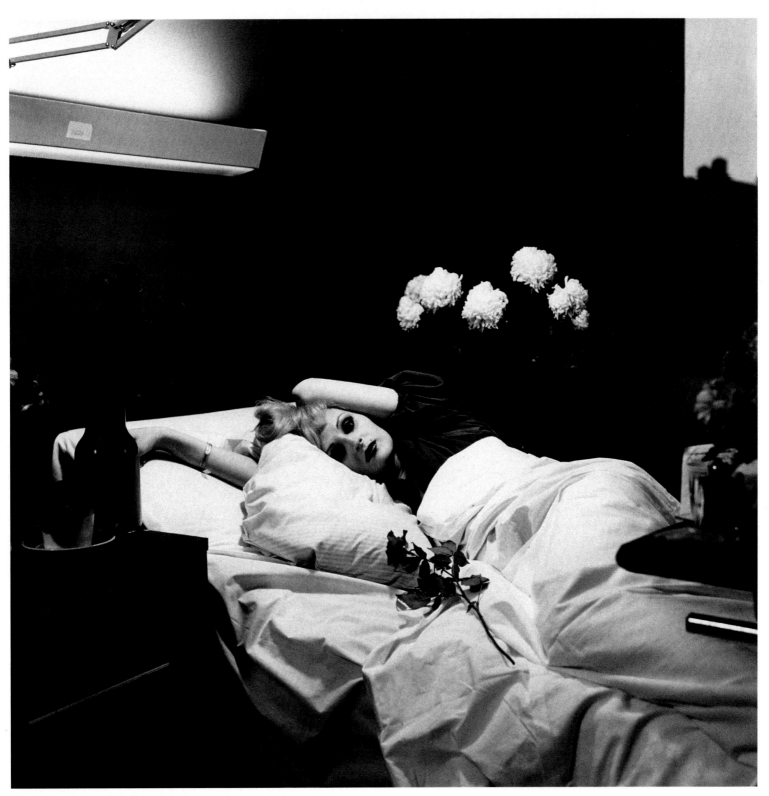

Peter Hujar, *Candy Darling on her Deathbed*, 1973

♀ MADONNA

The interview took place on August 25, 1998, in the living room of Madonna's duplex apartment on Central Park West. The space is large and imposingly formal, with oversize deco armchairs and a plush sofa across the room from a fireplace flanked by shelves that are empty save for a few deco vases and some art books. There are paintings by Tamara de Lempicka on two walls, a small, exquisite Dali canvas near the fireplace, and some framed photos of her child, Lourdes, on a sideboard. A book by the Peruvian photographer Martin Chambi sits on the coffee table, where an assistant has placed a tray with a china tea service, but the room feels like a public space, a meeting room for guests rather than an integral part of the apartment's regular domestic life. Madonna, fresh from emergency root-canal work, says she's a bit groggy from the gas, but she looks just fine in all black, and she moves quickly from subdued to playful to witty woman of the world. —Vince Aletti

V: I found a quote from your interview with Bill Zehme, when you said, "I'd rather own an art gallery than a movie studio. Or a museum. I'd rather be Peggy Guggenheim than Harry Cohn." Where did your interest in art and photography start?

M: My interest in art started as a child because several members of my family could paint and draw and I couldn't, so I was living vicariously through them. And from going to the Detroit Institute of Arts, which is how I got into Diego Rivera, which is how I found out about Frida Kahlo and started reading about her. Then, if you go to enough Catholic churches, there's art everywhere, so you get introduced to it that way, from a religious ecstasy point of view. And then just coming to New York and dancing. As an incredibly poor struggling dancer, you could get into museums for free, so that was my form of entertainment. It was just something I was interested in. And then you get into it, and when I started collecting, I started reading more and more about the artists themselves, and names would keep popping up—you know, Peggy Guggenheim. And of course I started reading about her and she was just—

V: She was definitely a character.

M: Oh, my God! What a life she led! Just the idea of being in contact with all those great artists and nurturing them and giving them a place to show their work and being their patroness is, to me, fabulous.

V: It's the one great thing to be.

M: Totally! I mean that's real art. And to be able to be a part of that and to nurture it—it's a very enviable and honorable position.

V: I've always collected images and torn pages out of magazines and put them up on the wall—

M: Totally.

V: And one picture that's been up on every dorm room or apartment wall I've ever lived in was this Richard Avedon photo of Lew Alcindor from Harper's *Bazaar*. I wondered if there was anything like that in your life early on. Was there an image that you've carried with you?

M: The image that always struck me was one that I ended up using as an inspriation for one of my videos, and that's a really sort of Cubist photograph—I forget who the photographer is—of a man working on some big, huge piston-shaped cylinder.

V: The famous Lewis Hine photo.

M: Right. Well, that ended up in my "Express Yourself" video; that was totally the inspiration for that. Every video I've ever done has been inspired by some painting or some work of art.

V: That's what I was wondering. Obviously "Vogue," with the Horst references, which I know you got into some trouble for.

M: Well those were all pretty obvious. I consider them to be hommages of course. And I didn't get into trouble, the director did. Fortunately, I owned the Tamara de Lempicka painting that I used for the opening of "Open Your Heart." That one over there. Only we put lights on her nipples.

V: What else? Most of the others aren't quite so—

M: Obvious? Well my "Bedtime Story" video was completely inspired by all the female surrealist painters like Leonora Carrington and Remedios Varo. There's that one shot where my hands are up in the air and stars are spinning around me. And me flying through the hallway with my hair trailing behind me, the birds flying out of my open robe—all of those images were an hommage to female surrealist painters; there's a little bit of Frida Kahlo in there, too. What else? The "Frozen" video was totally inspired by Martha Graham—I have a lot of photographs of her dancing: the big skirts and all the iron shapes and stuff like that.

V: I thought that the "Vogue" video was especially terrific because those were all pictures that—

M: We brought to life.

V: Yeah, and it angered me that Horst couldn't see that as a tribute. What could be better?

M: Yeah, and those images are really powerful, and it's great to remind people of them and to bring it into pop culture and not keep it so outside where people are never going to be exposed to it.

V: When did you start collecting?

M: When I got my first paycheck, $5,000 or something.

V: Do you remember what you bought?

M: This is a good question for my art dealer. I bought a Leger and I bought a Frida Kahlo self-portrait, but I don't know which came first. But I remember buying it and I had just gotten married and it looked completely out of place in my house in Malibu. (*She laughs in a light, breathy burst.*) But those were my first paintings.

V: And were those things that you had always wanted—always hoped to have?

M: Well I've always been kind of obsessed with Frida Kahlo, so I was really into the idea of getting something that belonged to her. And then from Frida Kahlo I found out about Tina Modotti and then I started collecting her stuff and Edward Weston, and one person always leads to another person with me, because for me it started with Diego Rivera, then it went to Frida Kahlo, then it went to Tina, and Edward and . . . (*She trails off.*) Also, if you're into Picasso, and you want to find out about him and that whole area of art and European culture, then you start reading about Man Ray and the surrealists and Andre Breton, and all of a sudden you're in that whole world and you start having interests in other people. It's like a disease.

V: Of the best kind.

M: Lately, I've gotten more into newer photographers. I'm really into Guy Bourdin right now; I've got a couple of his photographs in my bedroom that I wake up to every morning. I just move all over the place, really.

V: That's been my impression whenever I read about the art that you have; it seems to be very wide-ranging.

M: It's more that a sensibility appeals to me. I'm really interested in two things in art. One is suffering, and the other is irony and a certain bizarre sense of humor. And that you can find everywhere.

V: Who else beside Guy Bourdin would you consider somebody new for you?

M: That I love? Well I love Nan Goldin. She's amazing. Now I'm into color pho-

tography—don't get me wrong, I still love black and white—and I like a lot of the really young photographers. I interviewed Mario Testino for his show in Naples and Rio, and he has a new book—it's great! Fantastic book—I love it. And I did a piece for him for the book and we had a lengthy discussion about young photographers that we really like right now. Like Mario Sorrenti—people that are considered fashion photographers. For instance, I love Inez van Lamsweerde. She photographed me for *Spin* magazine and she is unbelievable. She's Dutch.

V: What is she like? I'm really curious about her work.

M: She so interesting. She's tall; she's got really long black hair; she looks like a Modigliani painting. She and her boyfriend [Vinoodh Matadin] work together and he does all the art direction. They make such beautiful photographs, and they do a lot of campaigns for a lot of young designers.

V: A lot of their work looks very computer-altered. Did they do that with you?

M: Not that I know of, because I don't like that. I knew I was going to get it with. . . what's his name? I'm sorry I had too much gas and I can't remember anyone's name right now. David LaChapelle! Because you can't work with him without being computerized.

V: It's part of the look.

M: Yeah. Anyway, I just love [van Lamsweerde's] photographs, but I'm into Sean Ellis and Mario Sorrenti. Their photographs are very cinematic and they're like a whole new wave, I think, of photography that transcends fashion and Steven Meisel, Patrick Demarchelier—that whole school of photographers, who I think were really inspired by Avedon and Helmut Newton.

V: You brought up Mario Testino. I'd been wondering who would be the official pho-

tographer of your baby and he's not the person I would have expected.

M: Why, who would you have expected?

V: Someone you had worked with before, like Herb Ritts or Stephen Meisel.

M: Herb Ritts did take photographs of my daughter that are quite beautiful, two days after she was born, and those are all framed and in my house in L.A. But more like the classic, black-and-white; there are some beautiful, beautiful shots of her foot in my hand—incredible. There are some shots that look like photographs Man Ray did of Lee Miller, too. My hair was really blond and I had red lipstick on and they were black and white; just the way he processed them, they look very Man Ray-ish. But Mario's really one of my favorite photographers right now, which is why he ended up taking the official portrait of me and her together. And when she had a real personality; I mean, babies don't have personality when they're two days old. I suppose some people think they do, but they're just amoebas. They can't even focus on anything.

V: I thought Testino's pictures were wonderful.

M: Believe me, there's a lot more. He captured something about her. He has a real, natural kind of journalistic style of photographing that I like, which I think is better for a baby who's running around and can't stand to sit still. It's not about lighting or anything, it's about capturing her doing something, and he took some fantastic pictures of her.

V: It was those pictures that convinced me he was more interesting than I'd thought.

M: Have you ever met him? He is a scream. He's so much fun. He's the kind of guy who will photograph you, and if he doesn't like the way you're standing or something, he'll kick you. And he's constantly singing and

WITH ♂ VINCE ALETTI

45

moving around the room and he's so full of life, and I feel like his photographs are, too. He creates an atmosphere, a relaxed atmosphere, and then he just starts taking pictures. Which is very, very different than someone like Steven [Meisel], who is really precise. (*She says this last phrase with a deliberate pause between each word.*)

V: I suspected that.

M: He has a very specific aesthetic. But because I worked with him for so long, I felt like I needed to get away from it.

V: Let's talk a little bit about him, because I'm very curious about him and your relationship with him. It did seem like you two formed one of those bonds that a subject and a photographer can form.

M: Muse?

V: Yeah. And that you brought out very interesting things in each other.

M: Yeah, well, first of all I have to feel like I'm friends with a photographer and that we enjoy the same things, like the same movies, have the same sick sensibility. And I felt that with Steven, which is why we just kept working together and working together and finally the idea of doing a book together came up. You really have to feel like someone's part of your family to work on a book like that, where you're just like hanging out. And not only did we photograph everything, we also filmed everything on a Super-8 camera—everything that we did.

V: Really? What's happened to all that stuff?

M: Oh, it's around. It's in the archives. It'll be unearthed after I die. It'll be playing at the Film Forum.

V: What drew you to Meisel in the first place, and what clicked between you?

M: Well, first of all, he just really, really appreciates beauty, and he knows how to photograph a strong female. He's a diva himself. And he, like me, is sort of a scavenger who picks stuff out of things, whether it's old movies, old Warhol films. He's interested in street fashion. He picks up stuff from all over the place and puts it in his work and so do I. And he likes a lot of the same things I like. I don't know—we just clicked. He's one of those people who will call you and go, You've gotta see this movie

or rent this movie. It's always movies you have to go and rent or buy somewhere; it's nothing that's out, nothing modern.

V: He fascinates me because there's always what's there on the surface and then there's all this stuff behind it. I know he has this incredibly broad range of things that he pulls from, and they're never what I'm expecting next.

M: No, and that's the great thing about Steven. He'll take you down a road and then he'll completely throw a curve ball. I wish he'd do more outside of *Vogue* magazine. I suppose he can't. Because that's certainly working within a serious restriction, and unfortunately *Vogue* has turned into a *Speigel* catalogue.

V: I hardly pay attention to his work in American *Vogue*, because—

M: It's all about Italian *Vogue*.

V: That's so great, and it does seem that he can get away with just about anything there. But I am curious about the *Sex* book and how that came about. A lot of the visual influences there seem to be Man Ray and experimental European work.

M: Man Ray and every movie that Visconti ever made starring Helmut Berger and—did you see *The Damned*?—Ingrid Thulin. I mean I *was* Ingrid Thulin for several of those photographs. And the book was inspired by all kinds of things: those old Warhol films, where people did nothing and just sat there and peeled bananas and stuff, to all the Visconti stuff, especially the stuff we shot at the Gaiety when I'm dressed in an evening gown and I've got all the men on leashes and I think Udo Kier is even in the photographs. We had to bring Udo Kier back—he's incredible.

V: Was the book something you concocted together or something you decided you should do and then you pulled Meisel into it?

M: We were always fooling around and doing stuff anyway—stuff that never made it into any magazines—because we were always working together on so many things. I guess it was my idea and then I pulled him into it. I mean, we had talked about doing a book together, we just weren't sure where we wanted to go with it and what

kind of a book, because I love taking on different personas and becoming and transforming and the whole chameleon thing with a twist on Cindy Sherman—something a bit more aggressive than that. I'm a big fan of hers, by the way. So originally it was going to be this thing of different guises, and then we used to go to the Gaiety all the time and we got onto the subject of sex and gender confusion and role playing and men playing females and women playing men and that's how the *Sex* book came about. Steven, like me, likes to fuck with people, so that was a big part of it, too.

V: With the public, you mean, or with the people who are his subjects?

M: Everyone, everything, at every level. It was about celebrating the ultimate taboo and also just having fun doing what you're not supposed to do. I mean, a pop star's not supposed to do those things. I'm telling you, I had the time of my life while I was doing it. Of couse, I got the shit kicked out of me for it, so it's a good thing I had a good time doing it. And I had fun. I don't regret it. The whole thing was like performance art while it was happening and it was a real throw-caution-to-the-wind, devil-may-care time of my life.

V: Can you imagine doing something like that again?

M: I don't know . . .

V: There's no point in doing that again, obviously, but . . .

M: I never want to repeat myself. I like the idea of doing something political and provocative, but I don't know what it would be. That's one of those things that you can't plan, you just have to let it happen.

V: I suspect that if you meet another photographer who inspires you in the way that he did . . .

M: Or maybe I'll do it with film; maybe it won't be photography.

V: In a sense, you did it with *Truth or Dare*.

M: This is true, and I like that confusion of is it real or is it not real? Is it life imitating art or is it art imitating life? Is it something that we planned that we filmed, or is it something that we captured? Because I'm telling you, the line starts to get very blurred.

V: Even when you're in the middle of it.

M: Totally. And that's beautiful, too.

V: Let's talk about Cindy Sherman. I know that you sponsored her show of "film stills" at the Museum of Modern Art. What is it that appeals to you about her work?

M: Just her chameleon-like persona—her transformation. What she's able to evoke—the subtlety of her work, the detail. I just think her stuff is amazing.

V: Do you own work of hers?

M: No, can you believe that? I've always admired her work, but the images that were available to be bought I wasn't that crazy about. But I really respect and admire her.

V: What exactly was your involvement in the Modern show? Did you actually put up the money to buy that whole group of "film stills"?

M: Yeah. I was a patroness. (*She laughs at her own pretension.*)

V: I like that idea; I think it's important.

M: It's the best place to put your money, honestly. I know it's good to get involved in lots of charities, but I think it's really, really important to do things that inspire people in other ways. Because people need to have their consciousness raised in many ways, and sometimes it's too easy to just give your money to something that you don't have any connection to. It's much more gratifying for me to be able to give money to tangible things, like to help keep a theater open, to a school, to supporting an artist in getting a show together.

V: How did the Cindy Sherman arrangement come about?

M: My art dealer [Darlene Lutz], she has relationships with a lot of people at the Museum of Modern Art. They come to me a lot and ask if I want to get involved with different shows. The only shows I've been involved in in terms of financing have been the Tina Modotti show and the Cindy Sherman show—that's it. You know, we chicks have to stick together.

V: And you want to do something that—

M: That I love—that I love totally.

V: To go back to photographers that you've worked with, I wanted to ask about Herb Ritts. It seemed to me that you had an inter-

Paolo Roversi, *Madonna*, 1994

esting, symbiotic relationship with photographers, both as a muse and as a great subject. And these people helped to create your image in a lasting way.

M: Yes, absolutely. And Herb Ritts was really a big part of that, especially in the beginning of my career.

V: What did he bring to the relationship that made those pictures so effective?

M: An innocence. Herb is one of those people who doesn't even seem like he's a photographer. It feels like he discovered it by accident in a way, and he has a real naivete about him. He doesn't really plan things; he kind of stumbles across things. He's got a real aw-gee-shucks vibe on him. He's a really innocent, geeky-nerdy type of a person, and I became friends with him. I asked him to photograph my wedding, and things went from there. Because I always have to be friends with them first, and they become part of my inner circle, and once I'm really comfortable with them, that's when things start to be created. And Herb was very much a part of my social circle. And Herb—Steven doesn't do this much, but Mario does it—they always have a little camera in their pocket. I mean, Herb and Mario must have a billion photographs of me in their archives—just of parties, hanging out at my house, coming to visit me on the sets of movies—that I'm sure will resurface someday, when I've been reincarnated as a camera lens. But there's a certain comfortability factor that came with Herb. And I'd never really been conscious or aware of photographers before, and, believe me, I'd been photographed a lot before that, but I wasn't really present. I didn't care. And, in fact, all the nude photographs that surfaced of me from my early days of modeling for art classes and photography schools and stuff, I so didn't want to be there that I removed myself from the whole process. I wasn't relating to the photographer, I wasn't relating to the camera, and it wasn't a relationship. I wasn't there—I was gone. It must be like what a prostitute does when they're with a john. I was not present. So, to me, the whole Herb Ritts thing was the first time that I realized that symbiosis, that exchange of energy and the creation of magic that happens from that exchange. A good photographer creates an environment for you to shine—for you to express yourself in whatever statement it is you want to make. And you do have to feel comfortable with people. I remember Robert Mapplethorpe kept asking to photograph me back in the day, but he scared the shit out of me.

V: Why?

M: I don't know why, he just did.

V: You seem relatively unscareable.

M: Yeah, but there was some energy that he had that I didn't feel comfortable with. And I couldn't even explain to you what it was. I was very young when I met him and I hadn't been living in New York that long. Anyway, Herb was the first photographer that I really had a relationship with.

V: And then Meisel after that?

M: Pretty much. I worked with other people, but nobody that made a difference. And then I worked with Steven. What was the first thing I did with him? I don't even remember. But I remember once I got more into fashion and started collecting more art and becoming a lot more aware of the intersection of art and fashion, that's when I got into Steven Meisel.

V: In a sense, you were more on his wavelength, then.

M: I sort of went into Steven's wavelength, and then that worked for a while, too, and culminated in the *Sex* book and all of that stuff. And then I didn't want to have my photograph taken for a really long time, and then I hooked up with Mario Testino. I worked with lots of photographers inbetween, but a sort of artist-muse relationship existed with those three photographers.

V: There are tons of other pictures of you—

M: But those were just one-offs.

V: —but those were the photographers who seemed to bring you out in a collaborative way. Is there one, definitive Madonna picture?

M: I think there is with each photographer, but there isn't just one, because I feel like I change and evolve so much that it's hard for me to put my finger on one.

V: I suspected that you'd say that, because if you chose one, you'd be pinning yourself down to just one moment and there is really no one moment. Are there other photographers that you'd like to work with?

M: Like to become the muse of? Well, I really wanted to have my picture taken by Helmut Newton, and I did. I love his stuff, too. But I didn't have a relationship with him; he's not available, or accessible. I also had my photograph taken by this other photographer who I adored, but the photographs never got used: Paolo Roversi, he does beautiful work. They were going to be pictures for my album cover—not this record but the

You might feel intimidated by a woman who walked around in a pin-striped suit with her tits hanging out, grabbing her crotch—who absolutely doesn't need you for anything.

record before—but the people at the record company were all too freaked out; they thought the pictures were too blurry, they weren't going to read well—whatever.

V: In all of photographic history, who would you wish to have photographed you?

M: Well, Man Ray—no question, no question. There are a lot of photographers that I admire, but I'm not sure that I would have wanted them to photograph me. Irving Penn, but not now—forty years ago. I can't think of anyone else.

V: Weston?

M: Yeah, yeah. No question; he was amazing. But I think that's it: Weston, Man Ray, and Irving Penn—not a shabby crowd.

V: Following that, who in the history of art would you like to have painted your portrait?

M: Wow! That's a good question. Well, Picasso would have been amazing. I've got a portrait of Dora Maar that's *un*-believable. It wouldn't have been a pretty picture, but we would have liked it anyway.

V: With Picasso it would have been so beyond just having your picture done.

M: He paints your personality, he doesn't paint your portrait; and he paints his personality, too. But I'm happy to share a canvas with Picasso. I would have loved Bouguereau to paint my portrait, because I would have looked really good. (*She laughs*) He doesn't paint an ugly picture of anyone. Or Rembrandt, he would have been OK. (*Said with the feigned unconcern, and sly smile, of a princess indulging in high nobless oblige. Then, after a long pause:*) Oh, I know who: Edward Hopper. Love his paintings.

V: With your photographs, your videos, and your performances you've had a real impact on our ideas about femininity and, I think, masculinity because of the way you've pulled that into it. I'm curious about what influences you've had on your ideas about femininity and masculinity over the years. What were the defining influences, if there are any?

M: I think a lot of the art that I have has influenced me in that way. I have a photograph in my office that Man Ray did of Lee Miller kissing another woman that I think is really powerful and that has really inspired me. I've also been inspired by—well, everything inspires me. A lot of the movies have inspired me—a lot of the movies of Visconti and Pasolini. With Pasolini, there's a lot of religious ecstasy intertwined with sexual ecstasy, and when I think of Visconti's films, I always feel sexually confused by them. For instance, did you see *The Night Porter*?

V: No.

M: You haven't seen it? (*She slaps a pillow like a disapproving school mistress.*) Anything with Charlotte Rampling you must see. She is genius! Images of women dressed in Nazi Gestapo uniforms—the vulnerability and fragility of a female but the masculinity of a uniform, and the whole sense of playing that out and performing, doing

Claude Cahun, *Self-Portrait*, 1920

sort of cabaret—the movie *Cabaret*! The confusion: what's male, what's female? For me, David Bowie was a huge influence on me because his was the first concert I went to see. I remember watching him and thinking I didn't know what sex he was, and it didn't matter. Because one minute he was wearing body stockings—the whole Ziggy Stardust thing—and the next minute he was the Thin White Duke in white double-breasted suits, and there's something so androgynous about him. And I think androgyny, whether it's David Bowie or Helmut Berger, that has really really influenced my work more than anything.

V: You project so many facets of femininity very strongly so it's fascinating to me that androgyny is also part of the mix.

M: Absolutely.

V: That definitely comes out in the *Sex* book.

M: Yeah, but when you think of all the stuff that I did in my live shows with Gaultier and the costuming and having the two guys standing by my bed with the cone-shaped bras on. It's always been about switching genders and playing with that whole masclinity/femininity issue.

V: What do you find powerful about that—or intriguing?

M: I don't know—the most interesting people to me are people who aren't just one way. And obviously I'm attracted to it because I am a female but I have been described as being very male-like or very predatory or having a lot of male traits. But that's because I'm financially independent, and I have spoken about my sexual fantasies in the sort of frank and blunt way that has been reserved for men. And the more people have criticized me for behaving in an unladylike fashion, the more it's provoked me to behave in an unladylike fashion and say, I can be feminine and masculine at the same time.

V: It's seems to me you've always been about blasting away old ideas about what is femi-

nine and what is masculine. To say that you're not feminine because you take charge—that's an old idea about what femininity is.

M: And, by the way, artists through the centuries have been into role-playing. I mean Frida Kahlo always dressed like a man. And so did Lee Miller for a time. There are lots of people sort of switched back and forth, but that was always reserved for fine art; in pop culture, you're expected to behave in a socially acceptable way.

V: In a sense it's easier for guys—from Bowie to Jagger to Boy George—to fuck around with that.

Peter Hujar, *Vince Aletti*, 1975

M: Absolutely. Because men feel safe about it. Men feel safe with men dressing like women; they do not feel safe with women dressing like men. You're not feeling intimidated by a guy who dresses like a female, but you might feel intimidated by a woman who walked around in a pin-striped suit with her tits hanging out, grabbing her crotch—who absolutely doesn't need you for anything. Except for one thing, but even then, you can leave after that.

(Here, inspired by the film Elizabeth, *which she'd seen in London, Madonna digressed into retelling the history of Elizabeth I, including her unconventional life, her ascension to the throne, and her eventual triumph as a queen. She led up to this point:)*

M: But she never had public favor; it was a bit like the Hillary Clinton thing. She did all the right things for her country, but she wasn't ultimately revered. So she had a conversation with her confidant-adviser. She asked him, When have they ever looked up to or idolized a woman? Only one, he told her, the Virgin Mary. So she said, Then I will become like the Virgin Mary, and she did. She created a facade for herself; she stopped having lovers; she became like a virgin. She became sexless, and painted her face in a white alabaster way, and turned herself into an icon that was untouchable and sexless, and then she had everybody's respect.

V: At what cost?

M: I know, but for me it was a very enlightening moment.

V: But it is a terrible cost—to give up everything in order to rule?

M: Right, but if you are a powerful female and you don't play the traditional role that you are supposed to play when you get married and have a family and everyone feels safe with you, then you are going to be intimidating to people. And that idea has always been running through my work. Accepting it, not accepting it; accepting it, not accepting it. And shoving it in people's faces. I mean that whole crotch-grabbing thing was just so like, OK every other rock star in the universe has done it, so I'm going to do it. And you know how freaked-out people got about it. Whatever. But we got off the subject.

V: Is there an early influence on your ideas about femininity and masculinity?

M: I think probably my earliest influences probably came from the world of dance, especially with Martha Graham, because I studied at her school and I read all about her and saw the movies of her dances and performances. She freaked people out, too, because she brought to life all of these Greek myths and she reenacted them in her dances. And she was always turning things around; she was always the aggressor who trapped the men. And her dances were very sexually provocative, very erotic, and very female-assertive, and I know that that really influenced me. And also ballet is such a female thing, and when I was younger, being surrounded by male ballet dancers—to me, that's gender confusion. I mean, a bunch of guys walking around in tights putting their toes up in the air, and they're incredibly effeminite men. Being surrounded by that on a regular basis when I was growing up—I mean, I wanted to be a boy when I was growing up because I was in love with all of the male dancers I knew and they were all gay. And I thought, Well, if I was a boy, they'd love me. So I got into role-playing then. That's where it began. I remember when I was still in high school, I had cut my hair off really short, and I was totally anorexic—I had no boobs—and I would dress like a boy and go to gay clubs and my goal was to trick men into thinking I was a boy.

V: Did it ever work?

M: It did actually, a few times. Yeah, it really started in the dance world.

V: And when you got into music, it wasn't in the rock and roll world, which is a lot more gender-defined, but through disco, which was much more fluid.

M: And I'm sure that's really influenced me, because from the dance world to the music world, my social strata was mostly gay men. That's who my audience was, that's who I hung out with, that's who inspired me. For me, it freed me, because I could do whatever I wanted and be whatever I wanted.

V: Knowing that your audience is ready to be fucked with.

M: Totally. Ready to be fucked with and certainly not intimidated by a strong female. So the problem arose when I left that world and went into the mainstream. Suddenly, there was judgment. But before that I was in my little gay cocoon.

V: But you certainly fed off the judgment.

M: Well, absolutely. As soon as you tell me I can't do something—And that's how I've always been, starting from when I was a little girl. The boys could wear pants to church and the girls couldn't. And I used to say, But why? Is God going to love me less if I don't wear a dress? It just irked me—the rules. So I would puts pants on under my dress, just to fuck with my father. And after church, I would tell him I had pants and I'd say, See, lightning did not strike me. And I guess I've been doing that ever since.

V: Do you have a feminine ideal? Is there someone who seems like perfection—and I mean totally in your own terms?

M: Well, a lot of the artists that I collect and that I admire: Lee Miller, Tina Modotti, Frida Kahlo—that whole group of females that kind of started off as muses and became artists in their own right and absolutely worked in a lot of different worlds and moved in a lot of different worlds and were artistic and political and still had their femininity about them. I can't think of anybody now. That's a tough one. I'm sitting here and combing all the areas: Is there an actress? Is there a singer? Is there an artist now? Help me!

V: For some reason, Liz Taylor came to mind, but most of the stars around today are complicated because they've made so many compromises along the way.

M: Hollywood is about playing the game, and I can't think of any successful actresses who didn't play the game. There's a lot more renegades in the music business, from Patti Smith to Janis Joplin.

V: So Lee, Tina, and Frida, but neither of us can come up with someone working now who could qualify.

M: It's lonely out there.

V: Is there a masculine ideal, either now or in the past?

M: I would say David Bowie, absolutely. I was terribly inspired by him and I still think he's an amazing human being. He keeps pushing the envelope in his way. I can think of a lot of male artists that I admire, but everytime I start to think about them, and how they behaved, they were all real shits. Fuckfaces. And the thing is, all those women that I named—I know a lot about them. I've got-

ten into their work and then read their biographies and really followed them and studied them, and they're women that I really look up to. Whereas the men, I haven't followed as much; I haven't felt the desire to know about them. I mean, everybody knows what a shit Picasso was. But all of those guys—they were all pigs. I'm sure Man Ray was a pain in the ass, too.

V: But is there an ideal image of masculinity, one that doesn't depend on biography?

M: I got back and forth. For me, a male image that I'm really moved by is somewhere between the kind of Oscar Wilde type of a male: the fop, the long hair, the suits, too witty for his own good, incredibly smart, scathingly funny—all that. But then my other ideal is more like the Buddhist monk—the shaved head, actually someone who sublimates their sexuality.

V: Not exactly like anybody you've ever been involved with.

M: I wouldn't say that.

V: I shouldn't assume.

M: No. Like one of my yoga teachers, for instance. He has a Jesus-like quality to him. I know he's a heterosexual, he wears earrings and he's got a very androgynous look to him and long hair. But he has an aesthetic and a humility about him that I think is very appealing and something to aspire to.

V: Interesting. When I think of you and males, I think of all the guys in your videos, most of whom have been like thugs.

M: Hunky boys? Yes, I am attracted to a thug. I like that quality, but I like the other side of it, too. Because all guys who go around behaving in macho ways are really scared little girls. So you have to look beneath the surface. There's a difference between my ideal man and a man that I'm sexually attracted to, believe me. Therein lies the rub.

V: What is your overriding visual inspiration?

M: The crucifix. It's the first image that sticks in my mind from childhood. I've used it a lot in my work; I've used it in my videos; I've used it onstage. The whole idea of the crucifixion and the suffering of Christ is all kind of intertwined with masochism and Catholicism is a huge part of my upbringing, my past, my influence. And it's a very powerful image. ♂♀

Imogen Cunningham, *Frida Kahlo Rivera, Painter and Wife of Diego Rivera*, 1931

Above: Robert Mapplethorpe, *Patti Smith*, 1978. *Page 54*: Robert Gligorov, *Crinoline*, 1997
Page 55: Shirin Neshat, *I Am Its Secret*, 1993

Jaime Palacios, *Family Portrait #12*, from the series "Painted Ancestors," 1997

Ana Medieta, from the series "Silueta (Silhouette) Works in Mexico," 1973–77

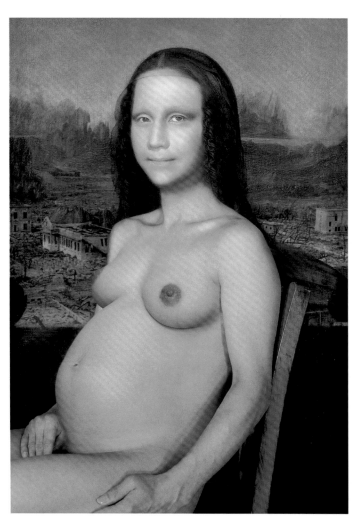

Yasumasa Morimura, *Mona Lisa in the Third Place*, 1998

Yasumasa Morimura, *Mona Lisa in Pregnancy*, 1998

Helen Chadwick, *Pram*, from the series "Ego Geometria Sum," 1989

Laurie Simmons, *House Underneath* (reclining), 1998

Mimmo Jodice, *Wedding Dress*, from the series "Eden," 1995

Top: Laureana Toledo, *Visto IV*, 1997. *Bottom*: Laureana Toledo, *Visto II*, 1997

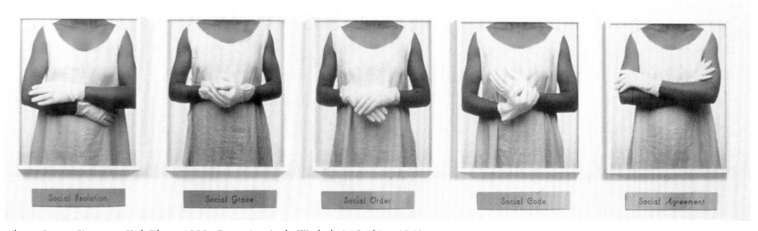

Above: Lorna Simpson, *Kid Glove*, 1989. *Opposite*: Andy Warhol, *16 Jackies*, 1964

200 ♀ WOMEN

Here is a short book entitled 200 Women. *Its prurience, considerable, is lexical and syntactic. Who is the subject? Who is the object?*

For an 8mm animation course in the mountains I drew a cut-out of Mae West and filmed her walking across a blank sheet of paper. Highlight was her gown's bell curve.

Sophia Loren performed in a sepia-tinted *Aida*, her voice supplied by Renata Tebaldi. Sophia Loren struggled to bear children, ate spaghetti in Naples, was youthful and

Dennis Stock, *Audrey Hepburn*,
New York, 1954

devil-may-care in a documentary on Joseph Levine, and bears consideration.

Doris Day grounds reflection, rode a swing in the credits of her TV show, was battered by James Cagney in *Love Me Or Leave Me*, defends animals, lives near Carmel, and wears dresses with French construction in *The Man Who Knew Too Much* while singing incestuously about what will be will be.

Patty Hearst rode in a car driven by kidnappers, had parents, appeared in *San Francisco Chronicle* photos, offered a cautionary tale, visited San Simeon, and knew Highway 101, which links cities in the South Bay.

Ida Lupino starred in my poem, directed *The Hitchhiker*, had a husband and a dis-

ease, saw Vivien Leigh in *Waterloo Bridge* and should have been considered for the part herself, was not in *Summer and Smoke*, and had Alexandra Del Lago aspects but was not pathetic.

Chance Wayne, hustler to Alexandra Del Lago in *Sweet Bird of Youth*, might also be friends with Montgomery Clift in *A Place in the Sun* when he wears an undershirt while working in the factory before attending a party in the presence of Elizabeth Taylor, who had near-death experiences and suffered comparison with Debbie Reynolds, who is not Doris Day.

Judy Garland sang "Hello, Liza" to her daughter Liza Minnelli, and knew Carol Channing but also knew herself to be Carol's superior. Carol Channing envied Barbra Streisand, who stole the part of Dolly in the film seen (and admired?) by Vincente Minnelli, husband to Judy and mother of Liza, whose sister, Lorna Luft, appeared in the movie *Grease 2*, not trumping Olivia Newton-John opposite John Travolta in the original. Olivia Newton-John sings "You're the One That I Want" as an argument for heterosexuality, and makes the act of loving John Travolta a divine pinnacle, an Eleusinian mystery, an anapest in an amphitheater. Brooke Shields appeared in *Grease* in its Broadway revival, graduated from Princeton, circulated with Bianca Jagger, was daughter to Terri Shields, wrote a book, and is not Tina Louise, co-star of *Gilligan's Island*, in which a character named Mary Ann appears, who has a family resemblance to Lesley Ann Warren singing "In My Own Little Corner" in Rogers and Hammerstein's *Cinderella* on TV.

Peggy Lee confused audiences of her TV appearances at 7 P.M. and must have been rivalrous with Julie London, who is not Julie Newmar, star of *Batman*. Julie London always appears sideways on her record jackets, is not the only woman to sing "A Foggy Day" with emphasis on the words "in London town," and appears on the

compilation *Bethlehem's Girl Friends* in the company of Carmen McRae and Chris Connor.

Carmen McRae is not the sister of Sheila MacRae and is not the husband of Gordon MacRae. I am not sure who Sheila MacRae is. Probably a television personality, like Kitty Carlisle or Arlene Francis, who is not Arlene Dahl, though the art of distinguishing the Arlenes is as complex as parsing the MacRaes.

Among my neighbors as a child I numbered Charlene, Doreen, and Noreen. Noreen's laugh, louder and stranger than Charlene's, seemed to contain the word "gefilte fish," though Noreen was not Jewish. No Arlene lived on our block.

Arlene Francis probably had no jealousy of Connie Francis, who had no jealousy of Connie Stevens. Connie Francis and Connie Stevens and Arlene Francis were three separate people with separate careers and separate erotic lives. Anne Francis appeared with Barbra Streisand in *Funny Girl* and was the star of the TV series *Honey West*, though Anne Francis lives in the Julie Newmar/Julie London category, where vocalism and TV fame blend to create a fog of anonymity and potential electricity that never crackles.

Susan Hayward played Biblical women like Bathsheba and was far superior in illumination to the Oscar-winning star of *Come Back, Little Sheba*, Shirley Booth, who echoes Shelley Winters: both played heavy

Dennis Stock, *Judy Garland*, n.d.

losers. Shelley Winters, erotic braggart, lords it over Shelley Fabares.

Shirley Booth bumps into Shirley Jones, who left the musical category to star in *Elmer Gantry*, for which she won an Oscar. Mother to David Cassidy, she paid attention to Susan Dey in *The Partridge Family* and appears in milk ads with Florence Henderson and some other woman. Florence Henderson starred in *Song of Norway*, the life of Grieg, and must endure the lexical nearness of Skitch Henderson, who conducted Anna Moffo in a New York pops concert in the late 1970s.

Who played Gidget? Originally, Sandra Dee, whom Stockard Channing spoofs in the *Grease* song "Look at Me, I'm Sandra Dee." Stockard Channing stars in the movie *Six Degrees of Separation* and resembles my friend Shannon who played Juliet in a college Shakespeare production. Eventually, many women played Gidget, though Leslie Caron, star of *Gigi* and *Lili*, never did. Nor did Julie Andrews, star of *Darling Lili*, though she played the same part in *The Boy Friend* that Twiggy later won in the film version.

Diahann Carroll is not Diana Rigg, though both appeared to great acclaim on TV. Diahann Carroll's Julia is not the Julia of Vanessa Redgrave, sister to Lynn Redgrave, whose *Georgy Girl* included the song I heard in the garage of my third-grade friend Mark, with whom I saw a double feature at Cinema 150 and got eye-strain as a result. The beige dress of Vanessa Redgrave in *Camelot* could be the outfit of Mary Tyler Moore in *Thoroughly Modern Millie*, in which Beatrice Lillie appears. Beatrice Lillie and Gertrude Lawrence are not the same, though Julie Andrews played Gertrude Lawrence in the disastrous *Star!* The beige dress that looks like skin recently made a comeback in the hands of Miucca Prada; my grandmother wore such a dress when she was Mother of the Bride to my mother in 1952.

Tura Satana in Russ Meyer's early sexploitation flick *Faster, Pussycat! Kill! Kill!* cripples a creep by driving over his legs. Tura Satana later became a nurse, I believe. Another nurse is Agnes Moorehead cater-ing to blind Jane Wyman in *Magnificent Obsession*. Agnes Moorehead washes her hands so energetically it seems a St. Vitus dance, and has a walnut-shaped face, like Myra Hess, pianist, who plays Schumann's *Symphonic Etudes*, certain notes of it, with frightening lightness of touch, so the tones dissolve into their context.

Charlotte Brontë was the subject of Elizabeth Gaskell's 19th century biography and was sister to Anne Brontë and Emily Brontë. The film version of *Wuthering Heights* starred the husband of Vivien Leigh, and the film version of *Jane Eyre* featured Elizabeth Taylor as the sickly Helen Burns. The Brontë sisters had minuscule handwriting,

Photographer unknown, *Vivien Leigh*, 1939

almost indecipherable. I read the Gaskell biography of Charlotte Brontë several years before I saw Elizabeth Taylor play Helen Burns.

Jane Fonda married Roger Vadim, who married and discovered Brigitte Bardot, who was a peer of Jeanne Moreau, whose lips are smoky and large as Simone Signoret's—rectangles, not ellipses. Jeanne Moreau's lips in Jean Cocteau's *Mademoiselle* are smudged and flattened by their criminal circumstance, as Bette Davis's lips are smudged when she plays the mother of Susan Hayward in *Where Love Has Gone*. Smudged lips are stretched, perfect, highly paid, and pleased by any technologies, including Cinerama, that bring them to the fore. Jeanne Moreau's mud-stained high heel in *Mademoiselle* need not fear the shoes of Audrey Hepburn in *Roman Holiday*; nor need Jeanne Moreau's shoe, clue to a murder, faze the ballet slipper of Judy Garland sitting on a stool as she prepares to sing "Born in a Trunk."

Joan Didion on the back jacket of *Play It As It Lays* makes me want to be a writer, as does Elizabeth Hardwick on the back of *Sleepless Nights*, and Jean Rhys on the back of *Sleep It Off, Lady*. Elizabeth Hardwick and Joan Didion write for the *New York Review of Books*, as does Susan Sontag. Susan Sontag was a friend of the French film actress Nicole Stéphane, to whom she dedicated the definitive *On Photography*. Nicole Stéphane, star of Jean Cocteau's *Les Enfants Terribles*, must have been a friend of Jeanne Moreau and might have been a friend of Arletty. Arletty and Colette might have known each other. I read Colette's *The Pure and the Impure* on an airplane and am not a child of paradise.

Victoria de los Angeles was not born in Los Angeles, sang Amelia in *Simon Boccanegra*, and recorded for Angel, which issued *Swan Lake* and *Sleeping Beauty* in a record with green cover in the early 1960s. Angel also issued Elisabeth Schwarzkopf singing the Verdi *Requiem*; in the "Agnus Dei" it is difficult to tell her voice apart from Christa Ludwig's when they sing in unison.

Maria Tallchief created the part of the Sugar Plum Fairy in Ballanchine's *Nutcracker*. Frank O'Hara idolized Tanaquil LeClerc, and Joseph Cornell made a jewel casket for Marie Taglioni, as well as pieces for Susan Sontag, Henriette Sontag, and Lauren Bacall. Henriette Sontag in the nineteenth century sang Donna Anna in *Don Giovanni*, as did Joan Sutherland, Leontyne Price, and Martina Arroyo in the twentieth. Joan Sutherland's repertoire included Mozart but did not center on it. She sang

Clotilde to Maria Callas's Norma in London in the 1950s, and has a son named Adam, who collects her records.

Miss Jacobson, my sixth grade teacher, wore a yellow dress. Miss Paul, my second grade teacher, wore flat shoes, as did Mrs. Leaf, my first grade teacher, and Mrs. Crandall, my kindergarten teacher. My fourth grade teacher, Mrs. Nigh, was short, as was Mrs. Leaf, and my fifth grade teacher, Mrs. Pratt, was tall, and introduced sex education while wearing a grey dress and pointing to her hips and saying "I have wide hips, which made childbirth easy." I asked Mrs. Pratt what happens if the penis gets stuck

Burt Glinn, *Elizabeth Taylor*, 1959

in the vagina during intercourse, and she said that wasn't a problem.

Mrs. Rosendin, my seventh grade typing teacher, wore her hair in a bun, and the school nurse in elementary school had an office down the hall from the school secretary, who handled tardy students and absences and also managed manilla folders.

Mrs. Hirose, my third grade teacher, her hair in a pony-tail, pulled down the pants of a boy who had been "bad" and spanked his naked rear-end with a paddle she kept hanging from a hook in the classroom, while the rest of us watched. She sometimes wore leis.

I read the first chapter of Jane Austen's *Pride and Prejudice* in sixth grade and gave an oral report on the whole novel though I hadn't finished it. My favorite girl in sixth grade was Cheryl, but she was not Cheryl Tiegs or Cheryl Studer. Sixth-grade Cheryl

resembled the daughter in *The Sound of Music* who went on to play a princess in *Lost in Space*. The princess moment took up two episodes and was a highlight of the series. My brother's first cello teacher, Cheryl, studied with Pablo Casals, and eventually became a nun, or tried to. She was a friend of my piano teacher, Lynn. Before Lynn I had two piano teachers, Mrs. Lincoln and Mrs. Shannon. Together, Mrs. Lincoln and Mrs. Shannon ran a music school, "Music Craft," in which I matriculated before kindergarten. Mrs. Lincoln was older or darker than Mrs. Shannon, who said my hands were too small.

Most things in the world are private. What I am saying now is no longer private. Once, I had complicated language, but the complications unraveled.

My Sunday School teacher, Miss Forkash, had a pretty face, but I can't remember it. Her signature on a certificate attested to decent conduct or consistent attendance. I learned about God's will and atheism and cut class to read a volume of great American plays including a Rodgers and Hammerstein musical that never entered popular consciousness.

The noisy behavior of the other boys in Miss Forkash's class depressed me. She told us that Jews let strangers—hitchhikers— into the house on Passover.

Metonymy, metaphor, allusion, and anaphora are friends of Elizabeth Taylor when she plays a Jewess in *Ivanhoe*. My mother's best friend, Marge, was not Jewish, though she had a tan and tolerated our contiguity: she lived in the duplex next door when I was born, and heard my infancy through the walls.

Shirley Temple, famous by the age of four, had curly hair, blew Deanna Durbin out of the water, and influenced the life of Margaret O'Brien, who is not Maureen O'Sullivan, mother of Mia Farrow, though Margaret O'Brien and Maureen O'Sullivan both played household roles. Mia Farrow must have known Mary Quant and Veruschka and Nico, though I can find no evidence.

Elizabeth Bishop, protégé of Marianne Moore, met Moore's mother, Mary Warner. Marianne Moore met George Platt Lynes,

who photographed her, and also photographed Edith Sitwell. Edith Sitwell met Virginia Woolf and Gertrude Stein, whose lover, Alice B. Toklas, met James Merrill, who met Alison Lurie, who lives in Key West, where I took a week's vacation and read the autobiography of Anita O'Day, who admired Billie Holiday although Holiday snubbed her. Diana Ross played Holiday in the movie, and, earlier, sang "My World Is Empty Without You"; the backup band sounds tinny on the K-tel record.

Marilyn Monroe inaugurated her life as celebrity by posing nude. Raquel Welch never did a nude scene; neither, to my knowledge, did another siren, Jayne Mansfield. Hedy Lamarr did a nude scene in an early movie, and it would not surprise me if Greta Garbo had one as well. Did Clara Bow, too, and Theda Bara? What about Vilma Banky? Edna Purviance certainly never appeared nude; nor did Mary Pickford, Constance Talmadge, or the Gish sisters. Silence was not exclusively prurient. It is likely that Gloria Swanson did a nude scene, but unlikely that ZaSu Pitts did one, though she committed an act of violent biting in *Greed*.

Jane Bowles's union with Paul Bowles was hardly a mere marriage of convenience.

Simone de Beauvoir was married to Jean-Paul Sartre. Janet Flanner was married to no one and dwelled in a hotel. I plan to read De Beauvoir and Flanner in the near future. Their sentences are strong.

Photographer unknown, Julie Newmar, n.d.

David Seymour, *Sophia Loren*, n.d.

Roland Barthes lived with his mother, Madame Barthes, and Maria Callas's sister, Jackie Callas, remained close to her mother, Evangelia, though the more famous sister did not. Zsa Zsa and Eva Gabor were on good terms with their mother, Jolie Gabor, who employed Evangelia Callas.

Katharine Hepburn played Clara Schumann in *A Song to Remember*, and I played Robert Schumann's "Fantasy Pieces" while in love with Andrea in 1976. To praise her to my father I invoked the name of Anne Sexton: I said it was important to live wildly. That summer I did not read *Of Human Bondage* though I bought a copy.

Frieda Hughes, the daughter of Sylvia Plath, is now a poet; I saw her poems in *The New Yorker*. I wonder if Helen Vendler admires Sylvia Plath. I admire Helen Vendler, who is as trenchant and encyclopedic as Pauline Kael. I am glad that Helen Vendler praises the poems of Adrienne Rich, whose book, *Diving into the Wreck*, inspired me in 1977, though I doubt that she would countenance my writing.

Oscar Wilde's mother, Speranza, was a poet, as is mine. John Updike's mother is a writer. Literature runs in families, and often through the maternal line. My father is also a writer, but I have been more influenced by my mother.

My mother as a young girl was fond of Shirley Temple. I do not know enough about the voice of Shirley Bassey to hazard an opinion, though Shirley Verrett's performance of Orfeo in the Gluck opera is magnificent. Shirley Verrett is virtually the godmother of my friend Maurice, and I heard Shirley Verrett sing Desdemona and Aida in Boston, in the early 1980s. Shirley MacLaine's psychic powers do not provoke laughter or skepticism in me; I read her first memoir while vacationing in Carmel in the 1970s, and, on that same vacation, saw *Red Sky at Morning*, starring someone who resembles but is not Katharine Ross, who appeared in *Butch Cassidy and the Sundance Kid*, the first M-rated movie I ever saw, on a double bill with *The Prime of Miss Jean Brodie*, starring Maggie Smith. The pallor of a nude female model's breasts in *Jean Brodie* had nothing to do with the darkness surrounding our car at the drive-in theater. That night a sibling had an "anxiety attack" (that is what we called it) and stood outside with my father by the concession stand while my mother and I watched the double feature.

In sixth grade I took Jean on a date to see *Airport*, starring Jean Seberg and Jacqueline Bisset. Later at that same theater I saw *The Andromeda Strain*, in which a flashing light catalyzes a dangerous epileptic attack. The date with Jean never led to a kiss, and yet she had a beautiful complexion, just short of ruddy—not incongruous with the taste of a Lorna Doone cookie or the sound of Jacqueline du Pré playing Schubert just before her illness strikes. The body of her husband Daniel Barenboim, as I imagine it, has some affiliation with Lizst's "Mephisto Waltz" as heard in the movie *The Mephisto Waltz* starring Jacqueline Bisset and Barbara Parkins, whose appearance in *Valley of the Dolls* as Anne Welles, the proper New Englander, cannot interfere with my sense of Annie Sullivan's stay at the Perkins Institute for the Blind, where she learned the skills that helped her tackle the problem of Helen Keller, played by Patty Duke, who stars in *Valley of the Dolls* as Neely O'Hara, based on the life of Judy Garland, who was originally cast in the role of Helen Lawson in the same film, but was fired (she never acted again), and was replaced by Susan Hayward, whose role in *I Want to Live!* as the doomed Barbara Graham won her an Oscar.

In that film, Susan Hayward on Death Row wears high heels as she marches to her execution. That corridor reminds me of the hallway joining the bedrooms in our ranch house in the 1960s. In the rumpus room or in my parents' bedroom I watched Shari Lewis and Lamb Chop; I preferred Miss Nancy on *Romper Room*. Miss Nancy and Shari Lewis were equally generous with their time: a half-hour. But they returned, the next episode, for another half-hour. The half-hours added up. Lucille Ball gave many half-hours, as did Vivian Vance. The woman who played Lucille Ball's mother, Mrs. McGillicuddy, on *I Love Lucy*—I can't remember her name—had a grudge against Ricky Ricardo, who was certainly dashing enough to seduce women at the Copacabana, though these liaisons never appeared

Paul Fusco, *Diana Ross*, n.d.

on the show. Lucy's daughter, Lucie Arnaz, played the Brooke Shields/Olivia Newton-John role in one revival of *Grease* on Broadway, I think, and must be known to Cher, as a client is said to be "known to Sotheby's."

I haven't said a word about Fanny Mendelsohn, the sister of Felix. Nor have I mentioned W. A. Mozart's sister Nannerl, or Yehudi Menuhin's sisters Hephzibah and Yaltah, or Vladamir Horowitz's wife Wanda Toscanini, daughter of Arturo. Wanda Toscanini Horowitz brought donuts and coffee to the fans standing on line to buy tickets to her husband's historic return to Carnegie Hall in 1965. I wonder if the donuts were glazed. ♂♀

Opposite: Mary Ellen Mark, *Smoking Twins*, Twinsburg, Ohio, 1998. *Above*: Elliot Erwitt, *Plaza Hotel*, New York, 1964

Man Ray, *Barbette With a Mirror*, n.d.

Cecil Beaton, *Paula Gelibrandt*, n.d.

Jacques-Henri Lartigue, *Gerda*, Hendaye, France, 1937

Above: Annie Leibovitz, *Marilyn Leibovitz*, 1979. *Below*: Gary Winogrand, *New York*, 1968. *Opposite*: Ron Treager, *Twiggy*, July 1967

Opposite, top: Tracey Moffatt, *Guapa* (Goodlooking) 1, 1995. *Opposite, bottom*: Tracey Moffatt, *Guapa* (Goodlooking) 6, 1995
Above: Robert Mapplethorpe, *Lisa Lyon*, 1980.

Tracey Moffatt

Useless, 1974

Her father's nickname for her was '*useless*'.

Opposite: Letizia Battaglia, In the Cala district, Palermo, 1980. *Above*: Tracey Moffatt, *Useless*, 1974, from the series "Scarred for Life," 1994

Above: Elinor Carucci, *Soap*, 1995. *Below left*: Peter Hujar, *Greer Lankton's Legs*, 1983
Below right: David Wanderman, *Under Dunn*, 1999. *Opposite*: David Salle, *Untitled*, 1980

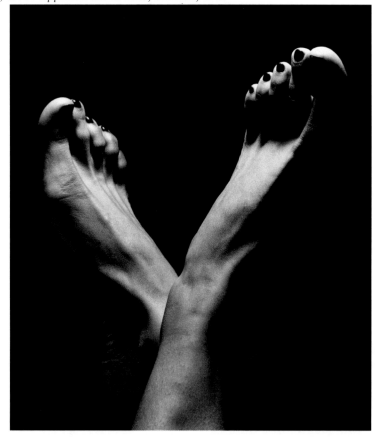

Above: Mariko Mori, *Mirage (E)*, 1997. *Opposite, top*: Cindy Sherman, *Untitled #275*, 1992. *Opposite, bottom*: Sandy Skoglund, *At the Shore*, 1994

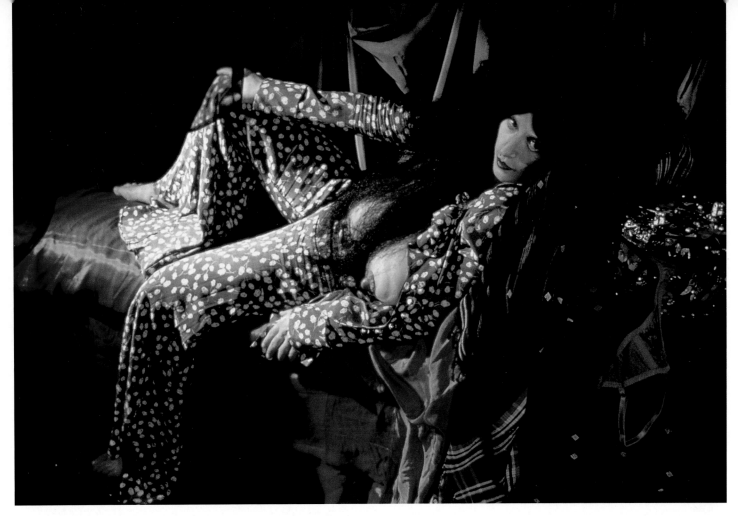

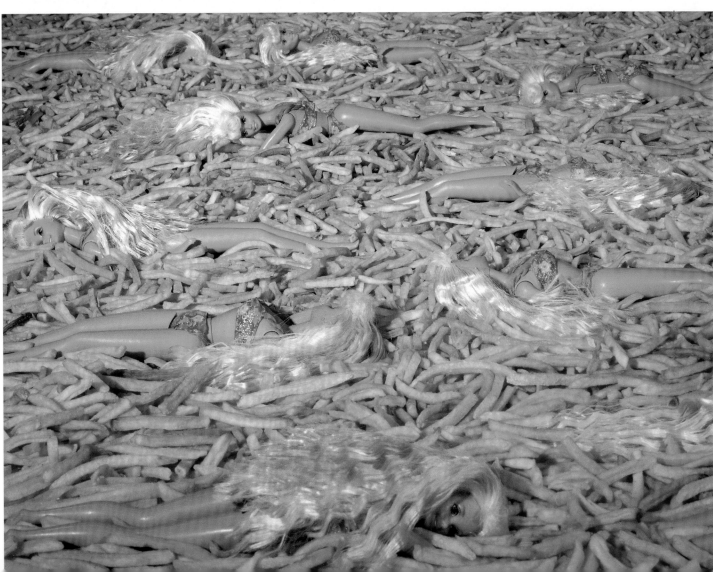

Clockwise from top left: Gyorgy Kepes, *Juliet's Shadow Caged*, 1939. Paul Strand, *Rebecca*, New York, c. 1922. Sylvia Plachy, *View from Parson's School of Design*, New York, 1976. Clarence John Laughlin, *The Masks Grow To Us*, 1947.

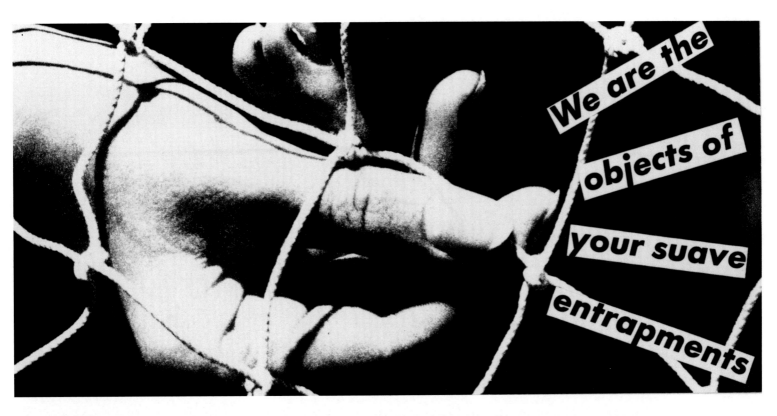

Top: Barbara Kruger, *Untitled* (We are the objects of your suave entrapments), 1984.
Bottom: Barbara Kruger, *Untitled* (We are your elaborate holes), 1983

Adrian Piper, *THE MYTHIC BEING, Cycle I: 9/21/61,* from the series "*Village Voice* ads," 1973

Carrie Mae Weems, *Untitled #2445* (detail), 1990

Philip-Lorca diCorcia, *Emma and Noemi*, 1992

Nicholas Nixon, *Bebe and Clementine*, Cambridge, Massachusetts, 1990

Mary Ellen Mark, *Tina Brown*, New York, 1993

Gregory Crewdson, *Untitled*, 1998

All images by Anna Gaskell. *Top*: *Untitled #29* (override), 1997. *Bottom*: *Untitled #21* (override), 1997. *Opposite*: *Untitled #5* (wonder), 1996

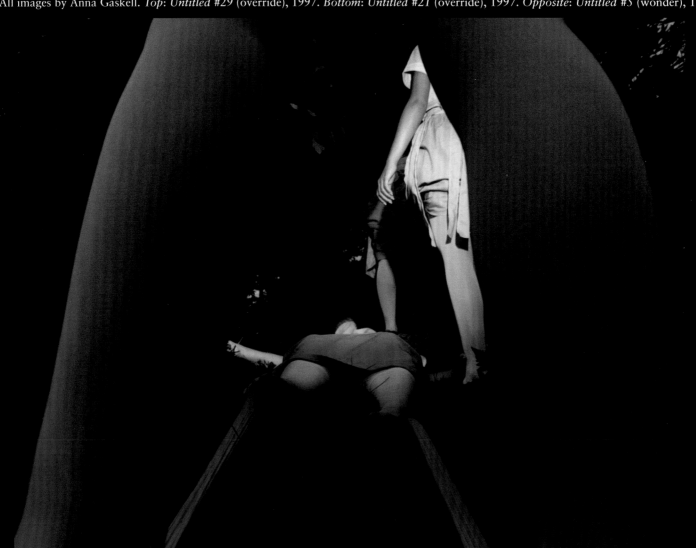

PEOPLE & IDEAS

FLIGHTS OF FANCY
Arthur Batut's Gender-Blending Composites

He's a comfortably stout man in a thick wool jacket, starched white collar, striped trousers underneath what appear to be waders, with a wool cape draped over his left shoulder. Atop his pale white head sits a wool cap; a neatly groomed moustache decorates his elegant, rather serious face. Out from under the cape poke two long thin lines: one a cane, or walking stick, and the other, disappearing off the lower right corner of the photograph—did I mention that this is a photograph?—must certainly be his shutter-release cable, for we are told that this is a self-portrait.

The subject in question is Arthur Batut, nineteenth-century inventor, tinkerer, photographer. He poses for his camera with one foot forward, a hand at his belt, and a resolute expression that suggests a man of the world who is prepared for anything.

Batut, whose works are preserved in an eponymous museum in southern France, boasts at least two significant contributions to the history of photography. To begin with, he made the first-ever automatic aerial photographs, in 1888. True, Nadar had made aerial photographs as early as 1858, by taking his camera up with him in a balloon. However, Batut one-upped Nadar by rigging a camera to a kite (the French *cerf-volant*, or "flying stag," is so much more poetic), and devising a means of opening and closing the shutter remotely by igniting a length of fuse rigged to the camera. The complexity and seeming imprecision of Batut's process notwithstanding, he produced some impressive results. His aerial photographs of Labruguiere, the village where he lived and where his museum is now situated, may not be staggering works of art, but they are clear, informative, bird's-eye views.

Indeed, kite photography remained in use for a variety of surveying purposes—situations in which a plane would be too high (or too costly) and a ladder too low—up until the Second World War. Today, hobbyists keep the faith alive: the Japanese Kite Photography Association mounted exhibitions at museums in Tokyo and Yokohama just last year. Serge Negre, director of the Musée Arthur Batut, offers summer workshops in kite photography in France and intends to offer them in the U.S. in the near future.

Batut's second, more problematic (and more strangely compelling), contribution to photography were his "portraits-types," composite portraits he made of groups of people in an effort to represent human typologies from specific geographic regions. Each composite was the result of multiple exposures on a single glass-plate negative. Seeking to capture archetypal regional traits, Batut made a composite portrait of ten young women from Arles, France; another of six women from the vicinity of Huesca, in Aragon, Spain; one of fifteen men from Laprade, in France's Montagne Noir region; and, most remarkably, a single, densely layered portrait of fifty inhabitants of Labruguiere.

In order to produce properly exposed multiple images, Batut underexposed the individual portraits by a factor equal to the overall number of exposures on a given plate. His subjects were all placed in the exact same position relative to the lens, with particular attention paid to where their eyes lined up. As a result, the final images are inevitably in sharp focus at the eyes and fall off toward the outside of the face. An eerie non-being with a distinct human presence emerges. For good measure, Batut also made single portraits, properly exposed, of each of his sitters, which allow for compelling juxtapositions with the composites.

These experimental images prefigured the first digital photographic composites by Nancy Burson, Keith Cottingham, and others by nearly a hundred years, and

Arthur Batut, *Self-portrait*, 1882–83   Batut's kite with camera

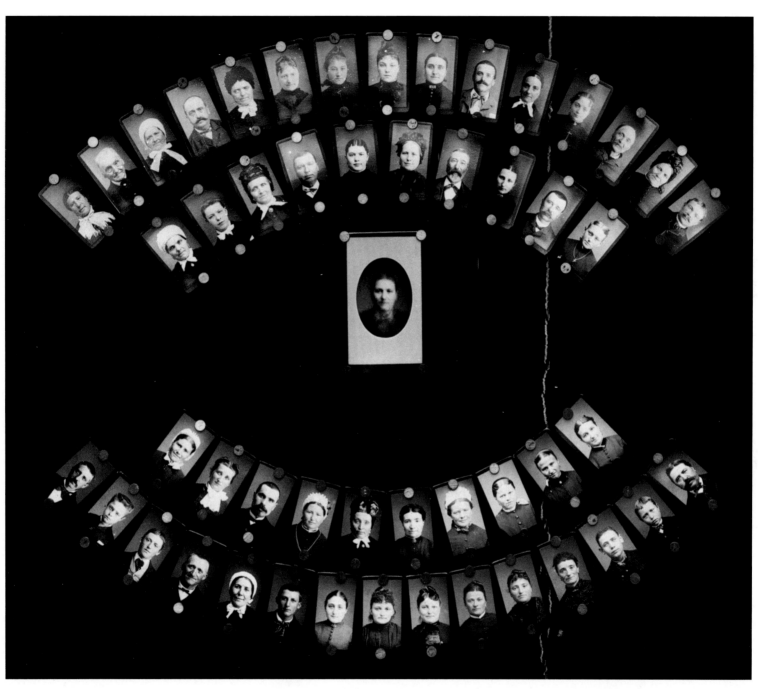

Fifty inhabitants of Labruguière and their composite "portrait-type," ca. 1885–86

Batut's writings sound eerily prescient: "To reproduce, with the aid of photography, a face whose material reality does not exist, an unreal being whose constituent elements are disseminated among a number of individuals, and which could not be conceived except *virtually* [his word, my italics], is this not a dream?" His composites were, however, very much a product of their time. Batut was inspired by the work of British biologist Francis Galton, founder of eugenics, whose exhaustive studies included the use of composite images to analyze character types and racial characteristics. Batut had no training in biology or ethnography, and was ultimately interested in something much more elusive—his own particular idea of beauty.

In an essay he wrote to accompany the announcement of his newly discovered technique,[1] Batut notes that his "types" exhibit a somewhat impersonal quality. On the other hand, he says, "they are always more beautiful than any one of the subjects who served to create them." Loss of individual characteristics, to Batut's eye, resulted in a generalized and idealized face. He cites the Venus de Milo as the Greek ideal of beauty and the virgin at the north portal to Notre Dame de Paris as the medieval ideal. The nineteenth-century ideal, he suggests, can be found in his homogenized photographic "type."

Batut was careful, wisely, to point out that his method formed a composite of physical traits, not psychological ones. Thus, when the Italian anthropologist, doctor, and criminologist Cesare Lombrosso attempted to use composite images to produce a picture of "the criminal type," or when a French magazine printed composite images of "the doctor type," Batut rejected such undertakings as spurious. Still, there is something unsettling in his idea that eliminating individual characteristics by means of photographic underexposure, and layering those ghostly impressions on top of one another, should result in a portrait that could offer clues to human similarities and differences.

That said, Batut's composite Arles woman does seem the embodiment of rus-tic, Provençal beauty. His composite image made up of six Spanish women from Huesca has a more somber, though no less striking, facial aura. She is also pictured for some reason against a murkier background, which no doubt contributes to what Batut called her "serious, passionate, mystical" physiognomy. And, of course, Batut was operating in a more homogeneous world than today's multicultural societies. If his portraits seem to have distinct regional characteristics, it may be in part as a result of the relative inbreeding of his society. In contrast, many of today's digitally altered portraits suggest a polyracial

"Portrait-type" of fifty inhabitants of Labruguière, ca. 1885–86

or androgynous ideal, as Michael Jackson's videos, the disturbing portraits made by Inez van Lamsweerde, and Nancy Burson's two composite portraits illustrating "the future of beauty"[2] exemplify.

Batut's composite of fifty men, women, and children from Labruguiere seems especially fantastical. In the individual portraits, we can see that some wear elaborate headdress, some are mustachioed, and that the subjects appear to range in age from roughly ten to seventy. In the final composite, the town of Labruguiere emerges from Batut's blender looking like a matronly woman with her hair tied back (all those hats and hairdos have disappeared in the composite), wearing a scarf around her neck (all those different collars), with a prominent nose and soulful, deep-set eyes.

What has become of the facial hair and the prominent cheekbones of some of the town's paternal elders? How is it that these "male" features have been rubbed away, like so many charcoal moustaches, to produce a "female" composite?

It may be due, in part, to the greater number of women in the composite—thirty-five out of fifty. Or perhaps the delicate features of some of the men (and most of the boys) helped tip the scales. However she came to be, our woman of Labruguiere looks for all the world like someone you would be happy to sit down to tea with, someone with a fascinating life story to share. She would probably turn out to be the local gossip, spouting many-layered tales of rumor and intrigue. After all, she's made up of a little bit of everyone in town. ♂♀

—MICHAEL L. SAND

1. "La Photographie appliquée a la recherche et a la reproduction du type d'une famille, d'une tribu, ou d'une race" (Photography applied to the research and reproduction of family, tribal, or racial types), 1887 and 1906, reprinted in *Le Portrait-type, ou l'image de l'invisible*, Ser-ahl Editeur, Labruguiere.
2. *The New York Times Magazine*, 100th Anniversary Issue, September 29, 1996, included two composite portraits by Burson on facing pages (pp. 162–163); one was two-thirds male, the other two-thirds female. Both composites were made up of photographs of the same men and women.

Photographer and historian Serge Negre and his wife Danielle discovered Batut's glass negatives and other sundry material in an attic at the house of one of Batut's relatives. Negre opened the Musée Arthur Batut in 1988. The Musée is at 9 ter, Boulevard Gambetta, 81290 Labruguiere, France. Tel: (33) 05 63 70 34 01. Fax: (33) 05 63 50 22 18.

For further information on Negre's kite-photography workshops, contact Atelier Le Bez, 81260, Brassac, France. Tel/Fax: (33) 05 63 74 56 22. E-mail: ArtLeBez @aol.com.

REMEMBERING HARRY CALLAHAN

A letter from Russell Edson, the fabulist, invariably contains some somber reminder: "There's always next year, until there's not. I don't think we would need to take our shoes off to count them."

So, now the obituary pages of *The New York Times* give us Harry Morey Callahan (1912–1999), photographer, born in Detroit. Gone. Damnation! "Gone into what/ like all them kings/ you read about," to quote a fragment of e. e. cummings's beautiful elegy for Sam Ward, the handyman at Silver Lake. Gone. And, Harry, me boyo, I wanted to tell you at least one more vintage Irish joke: "Why did the Irishman keep an empty bottle of milk in the fridge? In case anybody asked for black coffee." C'est sublime. . . .

I was blessed with an extraordinary collection of mentors: Harry Callahan, Aaron Siskind, Frederick Sommer, Henry Holmes Smith, Clarence John Laughlin, Raymond Moore; Stefan Wolpe, Harry Partch, Lou Harrison; Kenneth Rexroth, Kenneth Patchen, Edward Dahlberg, Charles Olson, Paul Goodman, Robert Duncan, Geoffrey Grigson, Basil Bunting, and James Laughlin. Lou Harrison is the only one remaining among us—active and vital at eighty-two in Aptos, California. You think about these things when you hit the Big-Seven-O. Just two weeks ago I scaled the stupendous heights of Gehenna or Tophet, whichever it was, and walking over the bonehills, I entered the portals of Genuine Geezerhood. Basil Bunting asserted very firmly that poets over seventy should be summarily ground into cat's meat. So, I have less than 350 days to dance and sing, friends and neighbors.

And, surely, some of these days will find me meditating on the intent figure of Harry Callahan, going about his camera work almost as in a trance. He taught by example, by pursuing the quest. Joel Oppenheimer insisted: "Be there when it happens; write it down!" Be there when it happens; click the shutter. Walker Evans, apparently, would say things like "If it's sunny, try f-16; if it's not, try 5.6." And "Remember, you push the shutter, don't let the shutter push you." Very Irish. I think it's just possible that Harry was from Nepal. But more likely from the Auvergne. Stick a beret on him and he looks the part. (In the Massif Central the mountaineers call berets by the word for cowpat, which I never quite remember.) Yes, in one past-life Harry was a herder of sheep, milker of goats, known far and wide in the hills for his kindness, his beatitudes, and quiet songs.

I've pulled twelve Callahan books off the shelves and I've spent some two hours ruminating, looking at the images and reading some of the texts. I had never noticed before this perceptive writing by Keith Davis in *Harry Callahan: New Color (Photographs 1978–1987)*, published by Hallmark Cards, Inc. "Proficiency in both golf and photography depends on sensitivity, balance, timing, and precision. . . . Both require an inward focussing of attention, and the ability to simultaneously think and feel one's way through the process. . . . In both disciplines successful "shots" are, to some degree, mysterious and unpredictable.... And both activities are deceptively complex; they are easy to do, but exceedingly difficult to do well." Harry used to shoot in the seventies. Good for him! As for photography, he said he'd maybe shot 40,000 images and liked 800.

Gertrude Stein said that when a Jew dies, he's dead. With Catholics, it's something else. *Laudamus te, benedicimus te!* Early on, Harry Callahan said: "A picture is like a prayer; you're offering a prayer to get something, and in a sense it's like a gift of God because you have practically no control—at least I don't." In a photograph by Todd Webb (1945) Harry looks very monkish. His reticence all his life aims toward the Cistercians, and maybe even the Trappists. Who knows? How eloquent he was when he said things like: "I love art because it doesn't have rules like baseball. The only rule is to be good. That's the toughest thing to do." Do the job, keep quiet. It was Jean de LaFontaine who noted: "By the work one knows the workman."

Harry also said that after he'd encountered Ansel Adams at a workshop in Detroit in 1941 he realized there were no mountains in Michigan, so he would have to look very hard at the ground under his feet. He loved walking. So, imagination makes me want to put him into a distant landscape with Matsuo Basho.

It's 1689 and Basho, the greatest of Japanese haiku poets, is about to set forth from Edo (old Tokyo) on an 800 mile walk to the Sacred Mountains with Sora, his friend and disciple. Time for Harry Callahan to change his garments, stick a 35 mm camera and a four-by-five view camera into his knapsack, master Japanese on the jet from Atlanta, bow to the Master, and call himself Sora. Let's listen to a few things they will say along The Narrow Road to the Deep North. I am using Cid Corman's translation of the text for the Basho. He comments: "We too move out with him to and through the backwater regions of Honshu. His words are our provision, breath, rhythm. And they can never be not of our time. The end of his journey is the end of ours. Everywhere he goes one feels a sounding made, the ground hallowed, hard won, endeared to him, and so to us, through what others had made of it, had reached, discovered." The information about Haguro-san I glean from the sagacious Jonathan Greene.

Basho: "O glorious/ green leaves young leaves'/ sun light"
Harry: "Michigan, 1912/ my parents were farmers/ no art, but/ father liked music:/ Caruso records"
Basho: "fleas lice/ horse pishing/ by the pillow"
Harry: "I was going to be like Van Gogh/ never be recognized/ and do this great stuff"
Basho: "quiet/ into rock absorbing/ cicada sounds"
Harry: "I never knew what I was doing,/ so how come you think you know?"
Basho: "cruel!/ under the helmet/ cricket"
Harry: "some talk about/ Far-Eastern thought;/ I guess mine's/ Mid-Western"
Basho: "cool ah/ faint crescent's/ Haguro-san"
Harry: "when I went there, it was with my heart,/ and I felt that they came with their hearts"

We leave our poet and photographer on Haguro-san, one of the "Three Mountains of Dewa" (along with Gassan and Yuduro-san) sacred to mountain ascetics known as Yamabushi. Past a famous five-story pagoda there are 2,446 stone steps up the mountain through very old straight & tall cedar trees. I hope to see you both there one day.

—JONATHAN WILLIAMS

Skywinding Farm, Scaly Mountain, North Carolina, 4/1/99

REMEMBERING
RAGHUBIR SINGH

Calcutta, Kashmir, Bombay, the Ganges, Kerala: they're among the subjects of the twelve photographic books that Raghubir Singh published before he died, suddenly, last April. Many years earlier, he once showed me some razor sharp images of interiors he shot with Kodachrome 25—his film of choice—in low light. The meticulous description he demanded of himself from such slow film could only have been brought off by the steadiest of hands. But Raghubir had a steady mind, as well. He always knew what he was after—nothing less than a photographic account of contemporary India, all of its cultures, whose ordinary sights he treated as glimpses from a vast epic. He persevered in that goal, bringing the look of India to Western attention, as no one had done before.

Self-portrait from the series "Mischief," 1999.

If you imagine what a Rajput miniaturist could have learned from Henri Cartier-Bresson, you'll have a glimmer of Raghubir Singh's aesthetic. His work was activated through density of incident, lightness of touch, and epicurean color. Motivated by a vision of his country's grandeur, this son of a well-born Jaipur family crossed immense social territories, sometimes under extreme conditions. He wanted his work, in writing as well as images, to be valued here because such was the only way he could make India known and valued. Everything else, practical and personal, was secondary to this odyssey of his life. It was carried along by what he called "A River of Color," the title of a retrospective book and show at the Chicago Art Institute, this year, visited by about seventy thousand people. Though his career was already prodigious, he had plans for many more books. An especially brilliant one, still in mock-up, is a gallery of primarily Indian streets, with the recurrent motif of his own face, as expressive as Buster Keaton's. This bonding with his native land was entirely typical, even though the book's title, "Mischief," signalled a point of departure.

—MAX KOZLOFF

Raghubir Singh's books published by Aperture include
The Ganges *(1992),* Bombay: Gateway to India *(1994), and*
The Grand Trunk Road: A Passage Through India *(1995).*

PARIS PHOTO

1999

The finest international galleries and private dealers showing 19th century, modern & contemporary photography.

Le Carrousel du Louvre
99, rue de Rivoli, 75001 PARIS

Opening night November 17th
from 7 to 11 pm
Opening hours:
November 18th / November 21st
from 11am to 8pm